PLANNING SCHOOLS FOR USE OF AUDIO-VISUAL MATERIALS

NO. 2

AUDITORIUMS

February, 1953

DEPARTMENT OF AUDIO-VISUAL INSTRUCTION
NATIONAL EDUCATION ASSOCIATION
1201 Sixteenth Street, N.W., Washington, D.C.

PRICE: $1.00

A PROJECT
of the
BUILDINGS AND EQUIPMENT COMMITTEE
Department of Audio–Visual Instruction

Co-Chairmen
Irene F. Cypher
A. J. Foy Cross
Thomas E. Batson
Kenneth L. Bowers
Lloyd J. Cartwright
J. Wesley Crum
Amo De Bernardis
Raymond Denno
W. H. Durr
H. E. Hansen
Ivan Johnson
Charles E. Luminati
D. F. Lyman
Russell Meinhold
Don Newcomer
Raymond A. Petrie
L. A. Pinkney
R. H. Shreve
Don White
Kimball Wiles
Harvey J. Woltman

Writing Sub-Committee

Irene F. Cypher, A. J. Foy Cross, Kenneth L. Bowers

Editor

Ann Hyer

Reviewers

Representative members of the American Association of School Administrators, American Institute of Architects, Association of Chief State School Audio–Visual Officers, Department of Audio–Visual Instruction, and other specialists in areas of schoolhouse construction were consulted.

Visuals

Visuals included in the handbook were obtained thru courtesy of the following sources. The figures refer to the pages on which the visuals appear:

Thomas E. Batson (8, 14, 20, 23)
Bell and Howell Company (13)
Kansas City (Mo.) Public Schools (16, 21)
Perkins and Will (Architects–Engineers) (10)
School Executive (6, 9, 11, 22)

CONTENTS

FOREWORD

The planning of a school auditorium is a cooperative undertaking. It involves citizens, the board of education, the superintendent of schools and his professional staff, and architects. In addition, the community would be well advised to secure outside advice from competent specialists on auditorium facilities.

A school auditorium is far more than a building to house a rather large group of people. In reality it is an educational tool or piece of equipment. It is good to the extent to which it helps to achieve certain specific educational goals, both for the school and for the community of which it is a part. In the main, an auditorium provides spaces for activity on a stage and for people to participate in various ways in the well of the auditorium. In addition, there is need for several small auxiliary spaces. All of these integrated areas, plus equipment, constitute the auditorium. A good auditorium makes it possible to develop intimacy and cohesiveness between those on the stage and those in the audience. This principle should govern both the size and design of the auditorium.

When an auditorium is designed with this principle as the guiding light, the resulting structure will really be an educational tool, and will provide a facility which will be used enthusiastically by the school and the community. Such an auditorium need not and should not cost a disproportionate amount of money. Also, it is an essential part of a total school plant. Rightly done, it is as necessary as any classroom or other facility.

This booklet emphasizes one feature of a good auditorium: adequate provision and facility for audio-visual aids. The suggestions it contains should be considered together with those necessary for other phases of auditorium use. The booklet does not attempt to take the place of the creative architect. Rather, it attempts to set forth the goals to be attained in order to secure good results in audio-visual activities. There are undoubtedly many ways in which the creative architect can achieve the goals presented in the booklet.

The proposals set forth in the pages which follow are constructive and should be extremely useful both to educators and architects and also to the lay public. It is a pleasure to commend to you this second brochure in the series.

Walter D. Cocking, Editor
The School Executive

THE WHY-Of Auditorium Planning

This brochure deals with the planning of auditoriums for the effective use of audio-visual methods and materials. It treats matters which are frequently overlooked or haphazardly included in planning auditoriums to meet today's requirements and tomorrow's needs.

Our concern is to insure provision of *basic performance standards* for adequate utilization of motion pictures, slides, filmstrips, radio, television, recordings, opaque materials, and display and exhibit materials for groups *larger* than the single class unit. These matters can be handled most economically and effectively at the time the auditorium is being built.

This brochure does not specifically mention performance standards for combination rooms, such as auditorium-gymnasiums and cafeteria-auditoriums. If such combinations are necessary, as many of the standards suggested in this booklet should be met as is possible. A small auditorium elsewhere in the school is recommended in addition to the combination room (31:93-95 and 32:94-95).

The auditorium is one of the major areas of the school devoted to the development of "large group" skills and appreciations, especially creative arts and oral and visual communication. The classroom is the normal place for most basic learning activities and lesson periods, but there are times when activities or meetings must be planned for groups larger than the individual class. At such sessions the wide range of instructional facilities available for single class use must also be available for the larger group.

For example, the activity might be an extension of some class project such as a debate or jury trial based on a unit of work in social studies and involving only the eleventh grade; a program by the school orchestra or by the dramatic club; or a sharing period in which Mary Brown's father shows slides the Browns took in Mexico to members of the seventh, eighth, and ninth grades. In some localities the school auditorium may also serve as the major community center. In such a situation an auditorium might house a community film forum series such as "Great Men and Great Issues." [1]

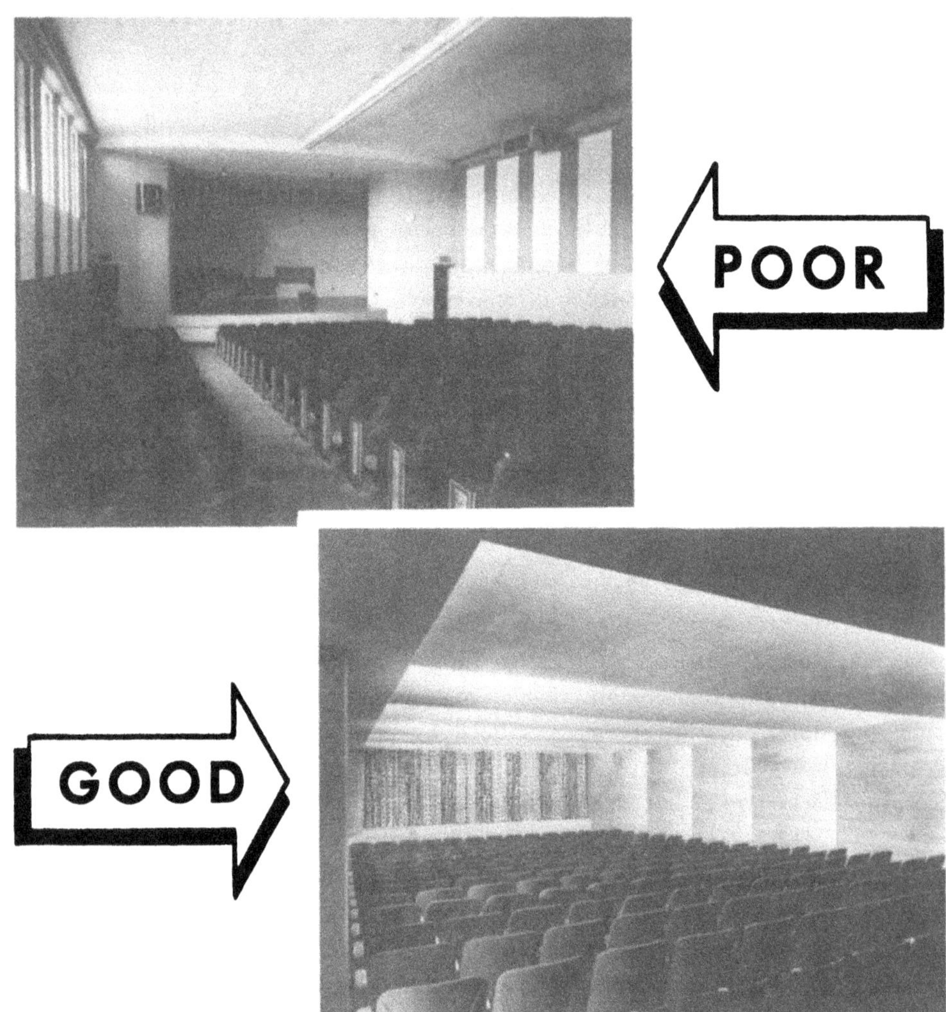

A contrast in auditorium planning, the good illustration showing a windowless auditorium, activity area with access to the stage and elimination of the center aisle.

These few examples have been given to illustrate the fact that the modern auditorium is more than a theater and more than an empty shell

---

[1]A series of adult discussion programs on "Great Men and Great Issues in Our American Heritage." Each of the nine programs is organized around a film presentation. The project was developed by The Fund for Adult Education's Experimental Discussion Project.

which can house a large number of people. It is a functional part of the school plant. Its existence is justified if it provides a common meeting place where groups larger than class size can come together to share experiences of many kinds--exhibits, demonstrations, displays, music, dramatics, forum discussions, lectures, motion pictures, radio programs, and many more.

The seating capacity and the shape of the auditorium should be determined by the type of program and the curriculum needs of a particular school. Those concerned with school planning should also bear in mind the relationship of the school building to the role it is expected to assume in the community.

A functional, well-equipped auditorium does *not* take the place of well-constructed classrooms in which adequate provision is made for utilization of all types of modern teaching materials and methods. In fact, if a school community cannot afford both adequate classrooms and an adequate auditorium, the classrooms should come first. On the other hand, a properly planned and well-equipped auditorium can greatly enhance the effectiveness of a modern community-centered school program. Auditoriums which fail to serve this purpose are little more than a waste of the taxpayers' money.

THE WHAT - Performance Standards

Seating Arrangement

A room seating 300 or fewer is considered a small auditorium, and one with a seating capacity of more than 300 is considered a large auditorium. The trend is toward the small auditorium and the handling of large group functions which occur only a few times a year, such as commencement, in a gymnasium, a fieldhouse, and the like, or outdoors (31:90).

In general, the arrangement of permanent seating in the auditorium will be determined by the size and shape of the room itself. In all instances, of course, the placement of seats, the number and width of aisles, and other details pertaining to safety regulations should conform with local building codes and with criteria found in the *Building Exits Code* of the National Fire Protection Association (27).

If possible, avoid a center aisle, as seats in the center of the auditorium provide the best stage- and screen-viewing angle. In a small auditorium it is wise to extend seats in a solid block and eliminate cross aisles. Under no circumstances should seats be placed up to the edge of the stage or platform at the front of the auditorium because free activity space is needed there. (See section on "Activity Space")

Whatever the seating capacity, the arrangement should be such that all projected materials may be viewed at no greater angle than 30 degrees from a line perpendicular to the center of the screen. This last condition is approximately fulfilled when no row of seats is wider than its distance from the screen. No viewer should sit farther from the screen than six times the image width nor closer than twice the image width. For some types of materials projected in auditoriums, such as motion pictures when no study of details is involved, satisfactory viewing may be secured at distances of seven and eight image widths.

In no instance should seats be arranged so that installations such as ceiling lights or stage curtains interfere with the viewing of the screen.

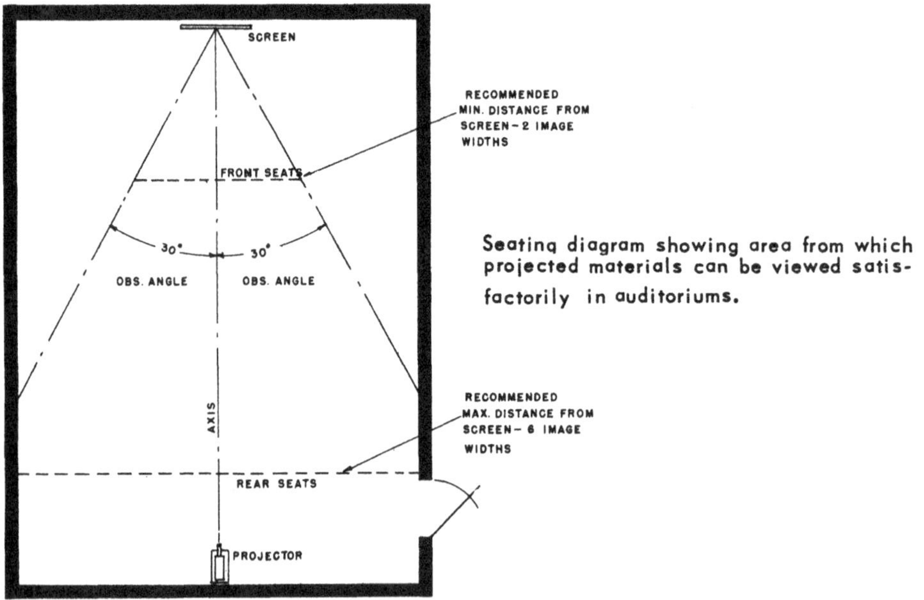

Seating diagram showing area from which projected materials can be viewed satisfactorily in auditoriums.

Activity Space

It is especially desirable that adequate free space be allowed both at the *front* and *rear* of the auditorium for small group activities. As in the individual classrooms, these project areas are essential for the group activities demanded by modern educational practices. The project areas should have easily accessible electrical outlets which are fused for 30 amperes and are independent of house lights or other fundamental circuits. Outlets should be placed so that no power lines will ever be laid across an aisle or a path to a doorway.

The activity areas at the front and rear of auditoriums provide space for many kinds of group activities.

The activity space at the rear of the auditorium is useful as an expansion area for activities originating in classrooms as well as for occasional exhibitions and as a free space for choirs, bands and audience reception.

A windowless auditorium with adequate front activity space.

There should be a relatively large activity space (15-20 feet) between the stage and the front row of seats. This space should be easily accessible from the stage as well as from the main floor. It is commonly used for music and drama activities, for exhibits and demonstrations, for small-group discussions and the like. Such uses require provision of electric current outlets, microphone and speaker outlets, a portable projection screen, vertical and horizontal display facilities, and sturdy, quiet folding chairs. Storage space for all such equipment should be provided in immediately adjacent areas.

A traditional lower-level orchestra pit is not recommended for the school auditorium, even if fenced off for safety. Such an area seriously interferes with the use of free space recommended above and prevents flexibility of movement for all small group units using the auditorium facilities. The front activity space can accommodate the orchestra.

The auditorium is not necessarily the place where only "staged" programs are presented. A stage or platform area is of course valuable for many purposes. However, not all groups need to perform on a stage. The auditorium will serve as a functional part of the school building to the extent that it meets the needs of the many and varied activities included in the modern school program.

Movable pedestal and block units can give flexibility to the activity area, thereby enabling it to serve the needs of many different activities such as drama, art or music.

Acoustics

Before spending any money on an auditorium, schoolboards should seek the guidance of a qualified consultant on acoustics. All too often, beautiful and otherwise well-designed and well-equipped auditoriums are relatively little used because of faulty acoustics. Acoustic problems cannot be solved simply by the installation of a public address system. Much more is involved in the creation of a desirable or adequate acoustic environment. *Even the best public address system will not correct basic errors in the sound treatment of an auditorium.*

An auditorium, like a good classroom, should provide a *comfortable* acoustic environment. There should be no strain on the audience because of noise or other unwanted sound, or because the level of sound is too low. Noise level for auditoriums should be no greater than 35 to 40 decibels (8).

In the auditorium, as in the classroom, the acoustic problem largely depends on: (a) keeping background noise low enough so as not to interfere with speech or music, (b) controlling reverberation time so that it will be short enough to avoid excessive overlapping of successive sounds and yet long enough to provide some blending, and (c) providing thru structure and equipment the optimum boosting of low-level speech and music sounds. Results depend on proper acoustic treatment of the room itself and upon the control of noise from adjoining spaces, from heating and ventilation equipment, and from the out-of-doors. Each auditorium presents a different acoustic problem, depending on such factors as the location, the size, and the shape of the room; the furnishings; and the number of occupants.

Audience noises and other background noises can be minimized and reverberation time can, for the most part, be controlled by room design and the proper application of sound absorbing materials on ceilings, walls and floors. The reverberation time of a room is the time required for the residual sound to die away to one-millionth of its original value. An auditorium may be too "dead" acoustically as well as too "live." An experienced acoustical engineer should be consulted to determine the required acoustic treatment for each situation.

The reverberation table indicates time limits which have been found to be acceptable in practice. The use of upholstered chairs helps to minimize the change in reverberation time with changes in the size of the audience.

Some new auditoriums are made acoustically alive without objectionable reverberation thru the use of long splayed walls and ceilings starting at the procenium arch and extending a considerable distance. These splays tend to reinforce the speakers' voices.

Volume of room in cubic feet	Acceptable limits of reverberation time (in seconds)	
	Half Audience	Maximum Audience
10,000	0.9-1.2	0.6-0.8
25,000	1.0-1.3	0.8-1.1
50,000	1.2-1.5	0.9-1.3
100,000	1.5-1.8	1.2-1.5
200,000	1.8-2.0	1.4-1.7
400,000	2.1-2.3	1.7-2.0
600,000	2.3-2.6	1.8-2.2
800,000	2.5-2.8	1.9-2.3
1,000,000	2.6-2.9	2.1-2.5

Reverberation time limits.

Sound insulation may be accomplished in part by skilful building layout so that auditoriums are well removed from noisy areas such as gymnasiums, cafeterias and school shops. Further insulation may be gained thru use of proper wall materials, use of floor and ceiling insulation, by careful location and insulation of heat ducts and service lines. The adoption of the *windowless design* will also greatly simplify the problem of creating a comfortable acoustic environment in the auditorium.

Ventilation

Provision for adequate ventilation is more difficult in auditoriums than in classrooms because in auditoriums such natural channels as doors and windows, if any, are closed for relatively long periods of time. While small increases in carbon dioxide and humidity occurring in stale air are not dangerous to health, alertness and comfort demand a reasonable supply of fresh air and relatively low humidity at all times.

Since each child represents a heat radiation surface, temperature control becomes important at all times, particularly so in warm weather. A sufficiently large area or number of ducts must be provided to ventilate the auditorium without objectionable noise or drafts in any section.

State codes set various requirements, often as much as 30 cubic feet of fresh air per person per minute, but a minimum of 15 cubic feet per person per minute is adequate for the removal of excessive heat and odors

(3:148). There is, however, no generally accepted formula for determining the exact amount of fresh air to be provided per person in auditoriums.

The control of the heating and ventilation system for the auditorium should be independent of the heating and ventilation controls serving the rest of the school plant. It is essential that sounds and vibrations from the ventilation system be insulated from the auditorium.

Wiring

The wiring for use of audio-visual materials and equipment in auditoriums is not costly nor is it greatly different from that normally planned for large meeting rooms. Oversights, however, are frequently made in the original wiring of new auditoriums. Simple but essential wiring, which can be installed at a relatively nominal figure at the time of construction, may cost prohibitive amounts if put in after the structure is complete. If the conduits are installed when building, the wires can be pulled in inexpensively at any time.

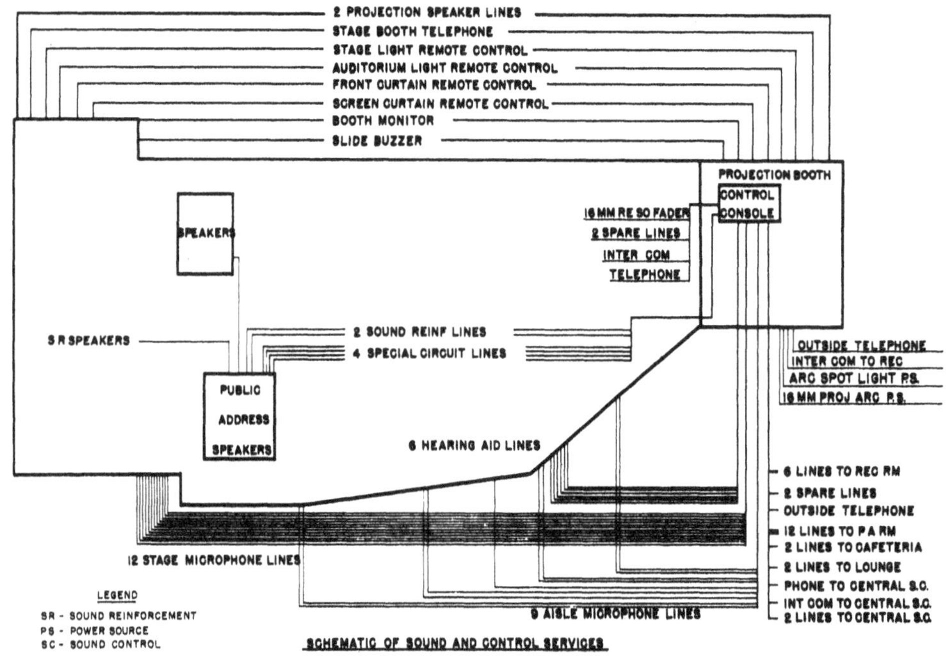

Schematic wiring diagram.

The schematic wiring diagram, included in this section, presents a more complete installation than will be needed in many schools. Care should be exercized in eliminating services lest the flexibility and usefulness of the auditorium suffer. Expansion and potential future needs should be considered at the time of construction.

Basic planning for wiring *must* include provisions for:

1. Electric current outlets (normally 110 volt, alternating current circuits fused for 30 amperes.) Ten such outlets should be located in the front activity space. All outlets should be independent of the house light circuits.

2. Speaker outlets for both permanently installed and portable speakers connected by proper wiring to projector stations, to the central sound system of the building, and to the public address equipment stations.

3. Microphone outlets in selected areas of the auditorium and at all projection, recording, and public address stations connected by shielded microphone wiring to the projector, recording, broadcasting, and public address equipment and to the central sound system.

4. Radio and television outlets connected by proper wiring to antennae.

5. Telephonic and/or buzzer communication lines from the front areas of the room to the projection, recording, central sound control, and to public address system stations.

6. Auditorium light control wiring (In large auditoriums both light dimming controls and controls for stage-curtains, window drapes, and projection screen are needed.)

Light Control

This brochure does not discuss ways and means of lighting auditoriums, but rather lighting for good use of audio-visual materials in school auditoriums.

Lighting in the auditorium should provide pleasant illumination adequate for the reading of notes and programs. A level of 10 foot-candles is recommended for those times when general assemblies are in session, or when an audience is assembling. At other times as much as 20 foot-candles may be needed.

Attention should be given to the installation of suitable lights to illuminate displays and exhibits, to center attention on the speaker and on materials he may be using, such as flip charts on an easel.

For motion picture projection, an over-all room level of one-half foot-candle is desirable, provided that not more than one-tenth foot-candle of this general room illumination falls on the screen surface. Aisles and hazards should be lighted with low level shielded light.

Research on the illumination of screen surroundings indicates that it is desirable to have some definite surround brightness (11 and 12). Surround brightness tends to produce less fatigue from viewing and quicker response to the image (22:438-439). Some suggestions for obtaining desirable brightness surrounding the screen were given in *No. 1 Classrooms* (13:10-11).

The control of light in auditoriums is most easily accomplished in those auditoriums constructed without windows. Where auditoriums are built with windows, there must be adequate provisions for darkening the auditorium for the projection of films and slides as well as permitting stage effects requiring darkness.

Drapes, properly installed, can give satisfactory light control in auditoriums with windows.

To control natural light in auditoriums where windows have been built, some mechanical means of darkening the auditorium must be provided. The most effective results are obtained by the installation of drapes, either plastic or flame-proofed cloth. These should be hung on tracks and operated by pulls so that they may be closed easily and quickly. If windows are used for ventilation, drapes should be hung so as not to interfere.

The drapes should be opaque and should fall within the brightness ratio standards of the Illuminating Engineering Society (21). Drapes should be hung with a metal or wooden housing across the top to eliminate any light reaching the ceiling and being reflected into the room. To prevent light leaks, drapes should extend at least one foot beyond the sides and bottom of the window casing. A center overlap of at least one foot also serves to trap light.

All artificial lights should be controlled from at least two locations, one backstage and one at the projector station or in the projection booth. In the case of older buildings, where the expense of rewiring is prohibitive, control can be facilitated by an inter-communication system or signal system between the projection station and the single light control station backstage.

It is desirable to be able to change intensity of the main auditorium illumination gradually. Sudden bright light or complete darkness is always disconcerting. This gradual change may be achieved by a dimmer control or by having groups of lights on separate switches so that a few at a time can be turned on or off.

Speakers

A qualified sound-system specialist should be consulted in the selection of speakers which will meet the demands of the auditorium under consideration. It is not sufficient to leave the selection of the proper speakers to the local "radio-man" unless he is an experienced sound-system specialist.

A minimum of two installed, high-fidelity speakers is required even in small auditoriums. Such "installed" speakers should be considered as expendable equipment, not a part of tho building. Speakers, like other elements of the school's sound system, should be checked at regular intervals and adjusted, repaired, or replaced when they show a loss in efficiency.

The school's central sound system, radio, public address system, and sound projectors should be properly wired thru a sound monitoring and control panel at the projection station in the auditorium. This control must be such that it can select or mix speaker input from any one or any combination of the sound sources named and should be equipped with a sound monitoring device such as a monitoring speaker or headphones.

For large auditoriums it may be advisable to add one or more carefully selected speakers to the basic two. Need can be determined only by analysis of the sound-boosting requirements of each auditorium.

While great care should be exercized in selecting and stationing sound-system speakers, no speaker or battery of speakers, however carefully selected and installed, can overcome certain sound difficulties arising from faulty design and poor acoustical treatment of an auditorium. On the other hand, the exact acoustical characteristics of an auditorium, however well planned, cannot be determined prior to the completion of the construction, decoration, and basic furnishing of the room. Therefore, it is well to withhold final selection of the speakers until the auditorium is completed. With the help of a sound consultant, however, the approximate location of the speakers (with provision for a maximum number of outlets) may be predetermined.

Projection Screens

Every auditorium should be provided with an installed projection screen. The auditorium screen, like those used in classrooms, should be of a type that can be made ready for use quickly and easily. It should be housed so that, when not in use, it will be protected from dirt and damage and be out of the way of other auditorium activities. A pull-down screen in a roller case mounted on wall brackets will meet these requirements effectively and economically for small auditoriums. Other types of installations, such as a flat screen mounted so that it may be raised from its viewing position *into a dust proof box or cover* above the stage, are satisfactory for large auditoriums. Large, tripod-mounted screens provide for small group use in activity areas and are valuable as auxiliary screens for small auditoriums. They are *not* recommended for general audience use in either small or large auditoriums. Roller screens operated electrically by remote control are very desirable in large auditoriums.

The screen should be placed so that no installation, such as ceiling lights or stage curtains, will interfere with the viewing. It should be placed so that its surface may be darkened regardless of time of day or outside light conditions and so that it can be seen readily from all parts of the seating area. Mounting the screen at the rear of the stage is usually not desirable unless the stage is wide and shallow.

Screen Types

Auditorium screens are of two basic types: the white matte screen and the beaded screen. Detailed information on the characteristics which should be considered in selecting screen types are discussed in such publications as *The Architects Manual of Engineered Sound Systems* (33:81-93).

Matte screens have smooth white surfaces. The reflected light is distributed more uniformly from them than from beaded screens. Beaded screens are covered with small glass beads which have a high reflective power. Although much brighter than matte screens along the axis from the center of the screen to the projector, the brightness falls off rapidly as an observer moves out from the center of the screen.

Stray light from uncontrolled sources, such as doors or windows, is "picked up" more readily by the beaded surface screen and hence complicates light-control problems.

Matte screens need a minimum of 10-foot candles of illumination and beaded screens a minimum of four foot-candles.

At extreme viewing angles, beaded screens show a greater degree of fuzziness or apparent distortion than do matte screens. If audiences are to be seated beyond the 30 degree angle or closer than two image widths, they can expect a less brilliant image and more fuzziness from a beaded than from a matte screen.

There is some indication that the observation angle for good viewing is being increased by the newer finer beaded surfaces now being developed. Before selecting a screen it is wise to have a demonstration in the auditorium under the conditions that will prevail and using the type projector which will be installed.

The unperforated screen is preferred for 16mm projection because of its higher light reflection quality. Also, 16mm audiences may be seated so close to the screen that the perforated pattern may be visible and therefore annoying.

Projection Stations

Projection Niche

For small auditoriums a niche or recessed compartment at the rear, rather than a projection booth, is recommended. This projection niche should be large enough to accommodate two or three operators with their equipment, and should provide a low platform which brings the projectors and the operators' line of vision above the heads of the audience. This recessed compartment should be connected with the front or stage area of the room by a shielded microphone cord and a speaker cord in conduits, in addition to light control wiring. Also at this station there should be not less than four electric current outlets, the outlet and room control for the school's central sound system as well as a sound control panel accommodating circuits of all sound equipment.

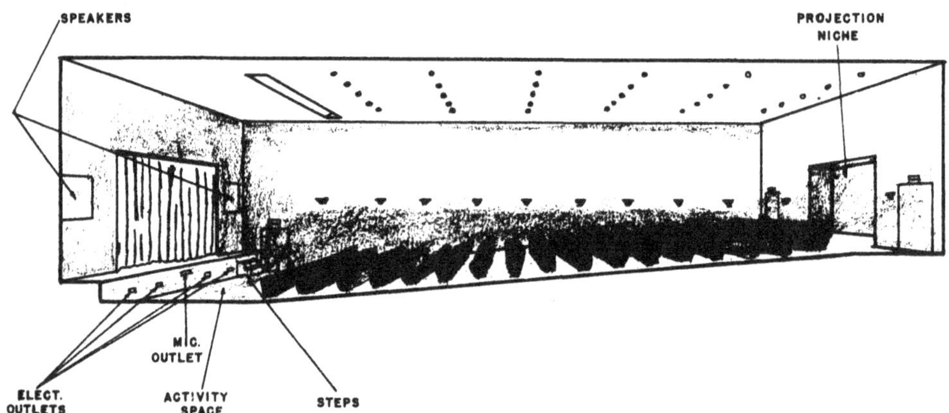

A schematic drawing of a small auditorium showing a recessed projection station and the flat activity space in front of the stage. Speakers are placed low enough to facilitate easy cleaning and adjustment.

Projection Booth

In the larger auditoriums provision should be made for a projection booth. The booth should be at the rear of the auditorium or near the front of the balcony whenever there is one. The projection angle should not exceed 14 degrees to avoid excessive image distortion. As a basic minimum the booth should have facilities for:

1. Projection of 16mm motion pictures. If sufficient funds are available, two 16mm projectors should be permanently installed in the booth to provide for continuous showing of multi-reel motion pictures. High illumination projectors are also required.

They may be of the arc type or of the newly-designed incandescent type with optical system constructed to give high-intensity illumination. If arc lamp projection is used, these provisions must be made: (a) fire-proof projection room, (b) direct current power supply for arc lamps, (c) a carbon arc exhaust system separate from the building and projection room ventilating systems.

Simple arrangement of apertures in the projection booth of a large auditorium.

Projectors should be placed so that they may be conveniently operated without interfering with or without interference from other equipment in the booth. Projection should be made thru soundproof, clear, low halation glass apertures. One or more additional soundproof apertures equipped with one-way vision glass should be provided for visual monitoring by the projectionist.

2. Sound monitoring and control. A small high fidelity speaker should be installed to permit projectionists, recording operators, and sound system operators to monitor auditorium sound systems. Such monitor equipment should permit control of the sound level on systems permanently or temporarily installed in the auditorium, including the school's radio, sound control system and public address system, and microphones.

Windowless auditorium with projection booth.

3. Projection of still picture slides. Slide projectors (preferably equipped for automatic slide projection) for this station should be provided with a high intensity light source and appropriate lenses. A projection aperture and viewing aperture similar to those described above for motion picture projection should be provided for slide projection.

4. Recording and playback of sound on tape at all common recording speeds and on three-speed playback for disc records. Recording equipment in the booth should be installed so that an operator may monitor by sight and sound any stage or other auditorium activities while making recordings or playing back recorded sound. Not less than two shielded microphone circuits should connect the booth with the microphone outlets on the stage.

5. Control of all auditorium lights.

6. Control of stationary spot lights.

7. Raising and lowering projection screens and opening any stage curtains installed in front of screens.

8. Communication with front area of auditorium thru telephonic and/or buzzer communication line.

9. Electric current outlets. Electrical outlets should be conveniently located and be available in sufficient number to enable operation of several pieces of equipment at one time. The outlets should deliver 110 volt, 60 cycle alternating current and be fused for 30 amperes. Lines serving the projection booth should be separate from lines serving the other auditorium areas.

10. Adequate ventilation and air conditioning. Needs will vary with the type and amount of equipment in the projection booth, for example, an arc projector requires an exhaust system separate from other building ventilating systems.

11. Storage of emergency spare parts, reels, recordings, etc.

12. Minimum maintenance and repair equipment such as film rewind and splicer.

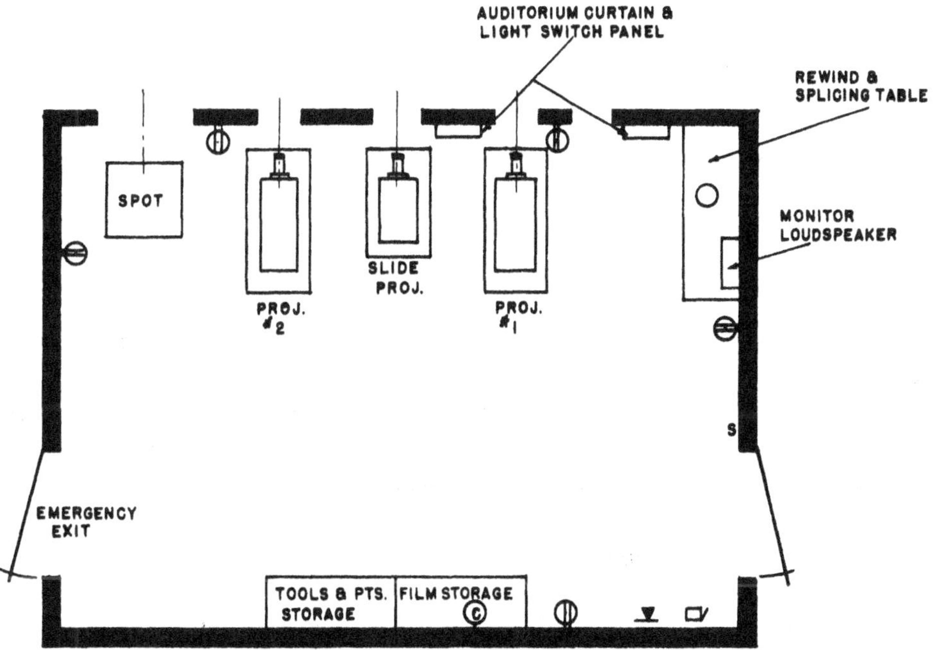

Diagram of the interior layout of a projection booth.

Other Required Projector Stations

In the small auditorium an additional station should be provided for the use of opaque projectors and other projection equipment which is limit-by light power or lenses to use relatively close to the projection screen. This close-up station needs to be equipped with only two electric current outlets, a speaker cord outlet, and one shielded microphone cord outlet with appropriate wiring to the room's speakers, and to the public address system and recording station at the rear of the room.

In both large and small auditoriums electrical outlets for a third type of projection station adapted to the use of the overhead projector should be provided. The use of the overhead projector requires an electric current outlet at or near the location used by most lecturers or speakers.

SELECTION OF EQUIPMENT

Who Should Make the Selection?

The audio-visual director, audio-visual coordinator, classroom teachers, student operators, and representatives of adult school-community groups should assist with the evaluation of instructional equipment. Actually, it is the "technical laymen," the classroom teachers, who are most involved in the use of equipment and who should be most involved in making the selection.

In the small school it is relatively easy to get all the people concerned together for demonstrations and selection. In larger school systems, on the other hand, a representative committee of these persons should be organized. In either case it is important that persons who have had considerable experience in using audio-visual equipment be named to the committee. Some committees have found it advisable to secure the services of a technical consultant. The equipment maintenance department in some school systems frequently can supply someone with a good technical background. If the district does not have such a person on its staff, often a parent with technical training in this area can help the committee. When sound equipment is to be appraised, an interested music teacher can be helpful in judging the quality of sound reproduction.

Some Suggestions for Organizing a Demonstration

Except in rare instances no selection of equipment should be made unless the equipment has been demonstrated under normal auditorium use. A few suggestions for organizing the demonstration are:

1. Have the demonstration in the auditorium in which the equipment will be used.

2. Use the auditorium screen for all demonstrations of projection equipment.

3. Use the same materials for all demonstrations of similar types of projection or sound playback equipment.

4. Allow the same amount of time for each representative to present his equipment.

5. Make provisions for equipment to be left after the demonstration so that the committee can examine it at their leisure.

6. Instructions for use and maintenance, service contracts, and guarantees should accompany each piece of equipment.

7. Provide each committee member with simple equipment appraisal forms.

Some Specific Points To Consider in the Selection of Equipment

1. ***Illumination:*** Operate the projector without film or material. Focus light aperture sharply on the screen. The screen should be evenly illuminated. No part of the screen should show "hot spots." If a light meter is available, meter readings can be taken at the center and at the four corners of the screen. Variations in readings will indicate uneven illumination.

   Equally important is the intensity of illumination on the screen. If screen illumination is too low, the picture tonal quality suffers and viewing comfort is reduced. Too bright a screen produces optical fatigue and a picture which is washed-out in appearance. The Society of Motion Picture and Television Engineers suggests a screen brightness of 10 foot-lamberts for auditoriums having one-tenth foot-candle general illumination (33:89).

2. ***Ventilation:*** Most projection equipment should have a fan for cooling. In order to check the adequacy of the cooling system, set up the projector and allow it to operate without projection material for at least 30 minutes. At the end of that time check

the projector for heat. If the cooling system is adequate, no exposed part of the projector should be too hot to touch lightly.

3. *Projector noise:* A point often overlooked in selection of projection equipment is the amount of noise made by the projector. A projector which is unusually noisy can be a definite distraction if not operated in a soundproof booth. Check the noise level with enough people present to simulate normal use conditions. Checks on noise level should be made from a number of locations with the fan running at full speed. Be sure to check from the seats nearest the projector.

4. *Sound:* It is advisable to have a well-qualified music specialist as a consultant to assist in judging the sound quality. Clarity, quality of sound, control of volume and tone, ability of the speaker equipment to handle the base range, and good volume control are some of the things to consider in checking the sound. For this purpose a film or recording which has a good range of sound, voice and music, should be selected.

   No appreciable hum should be evident when the volume is turned up half-way and the motor is not running.

5. *Simplicity of operation:* If equipment is to be operated by numerous "technical laymen," simplicity of operation is important.

6. *Maintenance and storage:* All equipment should be easy to clean, maintain, and store. Each accessory, such as slide carrier, arms, spare lamps and reels, and cords, should have a convenient storage place within the case. Projector case covers should be easily closed or attached when all accessories are in place for storage.

7. *General construction:* All equipment should be well built. Examine case construction, hinges, castings, slide carriers, lamp house, condensor mountings, sprockets, etc. The technical member of the committee can assist with this phase of the appraisal. All school equipment should be constructed so as to withstand a great deal of use and handling by many different people.

8. *Available service:* Unless the school maintains its own service

department, equipment which can be serviced locally should be selected.

THE HOW - Achieving Goals

First, involve all groups which are to use the auditorium, as well as building and equipment specialists, in determining just what kinds of activities the auditorium must be planned to accommodate.

Second, be sure that all such persons are aware of the complete range of activities that can be carried on in a modern school auditorium.

Third, justify the expense of providing the kind of auditorium requested in terms of actual needs expressed by potential users.

Fourth, acquaint those who must approve the cost of construction directly or indirectly with all reasons for the construction of desirable auditorium facilities.

A school auditorium which is conceived, planned, equipped, and regularly used as a large-group, common-interest center; as an expansion area for some types of class activities; and as an additional facility for bringing community resources to bear upon the job of education is an important asset in which most communities can well afford to invest.

There is, however, little justification for the relatively large outlay of limited school funds necessary to construct a school auditorium unless it is designed and used frequently for school functions which other fundamental school facilities cannot accommodate. Other funds and community resources should provide for any facilities designed primarily for community needs.

It is well to note that certain parts of a school program formerly carried on in a large auditorium may be obsolete today and many traditional and important school functions, while not outmoded, may be now more effectively and efficiently performed thru the use of such modern school equipment as the centralized sound system or television.

Flexibility is probably the most important characteristic of a well-planned school auditorium. Flexibility is essential if the multi-type, ever-changing program of the modern school is to be adequately housed.

APPENDIX

BIBLIOGRAPHY

1. Acoustical Materials Association. *Theory and Use of Architectural Acoustical Materials.* New York: the Association, 1950. 20 p.

2. Allen, Carl J. "Lighting the School Auditorium and Stage." *Progressive Architecture* 32:88-94; August 1951.

3. American Association of School Administrators. *American School Buildings.* Twenty-seventh Yearbook. Washington D.C.: the Association, a department of the National Education Association, 1949. 525 p.

4. Barrow, Alice, and Simonson, Lee. *The School Auditorium as a Theater.* Office of Education, Bulletin, 1939, No. 4. Washington D.C.: Superintendent of Documents, Government Printing Office, 1939. 51 p.

5. Beard, D. Max, and Erickson, A.M. "Auditorium Specifically Designed for Technical Meetings." *Journal of the Society of Motion Picture and Television Engineers* 59: 205-212; September 1952.

6. Bell and Howell. *Architects' Visual Equipment Handbook.* Chicago: the Company, 1945. 30 p.

7. Bell, Millard D. "Auditorium Central School, Wilmette, Illinois." *The Nation's Schools* 48: 52-53; September 1951.

8. Bolt, Richard, and Newman, Robert B. "Architectural Acoustics: Basic Planning Aspects." *Architectural Record* 107; 165-168, 244, 246, 248; April 1950.

9. Clapp, Wilfred F., and Perkins, Lawrence B. "Designing the School Plant for Multiple use." *American School and University.* Eighteenth edition, New York: American School Publishing Corporation, 1946. p. 69-74.

10. Cocking, Walter D., editor, *American School and University.* New York: American School Publishing Corporation. Annual edition. (1951-52 issue has an extensive index of articles on school building facilities.)

11. Cravath, James R. "Lighting Projection Screen Surroundings." *Illuminating Engineering* 46: 361-364; July 1951.

12. Cravath, James R. "Projection Screen Surroundings." *Illuminating Engineering* 46: 9A, 12A; September 1951.

13. Department of Audio-Visual Instruction. *Planning Schools for Use of Audio-Visual Materials – No. 1 Classrooms.* Washington D.C.: the Department, National Education Association, 1952. 40 p.

14. Englehardt, N.L.; Englehardt, N.L., Jr.; and Leggett, Stanton, *Planning Secondary School Buildings.* New York: Reinhold Publishing Co., 1949. 252 p.

15. Gillette, A.S. "The Auditorium for the Small High School." *American School Board Journal* 112:47-48; January 1946.

16. Gillies, Harry W. "Planning the School Auditorium to Serve the Community's Needs." *School Executive* 70: 19-22; August 1951.

17. Hare, Michael M. "Don'ts for the Secondary School Theater." *American School and University.* Fourteenth edition. New York: American School Publishing Corporation, 1942. p. 268-273.

18. Hearns, Edward; Jones, John; and Morrison, Jack. "Name your Poison." *American School and University.* Twenty-first edition. New York: American School Publishing Corporation, 1949. p. 200-207.

19. Hosler, Fred W. "Uses of the Auditorium In a Community School Program." *School Executive* 65: 34-35; June 1946.

20. Hunt, Herold C. "Factors which Determine the Size of an Auditorium." *School Executive* 65: 35-37; June 1946.

21. Illuminating Engineering Society and American Institute of Architects (sponsors). *American Standard Practice for School Lighting.* New York: Illuminating Engineering Society, 1948. 79 p.

22. Kolb, Jr., Frederick J. "Screen Brightness." *Journal of the Society of Motion Picture and Television Engineers* 56: 433-442; April 1951.

23. McCandless, Stanley, "Lighting the School Auditorium and Stage." *School Executive* 65: 45-48; June 1946.

24. Marko, Louis W. "Auditorium Acoustic Correction and Sound Reinforcement by Electronics." *Audio-Visual Guide* 17: 32-33; May 1951.

25. Maxfield, J.P. "Auditorium Acoustics." *Journal of the Society of Motion Picture and Television Engineers* 53: 169-176; August 1948.

26. Millgate, Irvine H., and Coelln, O.H., Jr., "Standards For Visual and Auditory Facilities in New Educational Buildings," *American School and University.* Eighteenth edition. New York: American School Publishing Corporation, 1946. p. 136-151.

27. National Fire Protection Association. *Building Exit Codes.* Eleventh edition. Boston: the Association, 1951. 136 p.

28. Nichols, John E. "Auditoriums and Stages." *School Executive* 68: 60-61; January 1949.

29. Olney, Benjamin. "Acoustics of School Building." School Plant Studies Series. *Bulletin of The American Institute of Architects* 6: 17-20; November-December 1952.

30. Partridge, E. DeAlton, and Millgate, Irvine W. "Planning the School Auditorium for Audio-Visual Education." School Executive 65: 48-50; June 1946.

31. Perkins, L.B., and Cocking, W.D. *Schools.* New York: Reinhold Publishing Co., 1949. 264 p.

32. Plant Guide Committee. *Guide for Planning School Plants.* Nashville: National Council on Schoolhouse Construction, 1949. 173 p.

33. Radio Corporation of America. *The Architects Manual of Engineered Sound Systems.* Camden: the Corporation, 1947. 288 p.

34. Schwartz, K.R. *Technical Considerations in Relation to Housing the Audio-Visual Program.* Bulletin of the School of Education, Indiana University. Bloomington: the University, 1946. p. 16-20.

35. See and Hear. "Designs for Visual Education." *See and Hear* 4: 16-24; November 1948.

36. Smith, H.L. "Trends That Affect Building." *Nation's Schools* 37: 35-37; May 1946.

37. Stanforth, A.T. "The Use of Auditoriums." *American School and University.* Nineteenth edition. New York: American School Publishing Corporation, 1947. p. 132-134.

38. University of the State of New York, Division of School Buildings and Grounds. *Planning the School Auditorium.* Albany: the University, 1948. 16 p.

BRIEF LIST OF COMPANIES MANUFACTURING AUDIO-VISUAL EQUIPMENT FOR AUDITORIUM USE.

(The figures following the company names indicate the types of products manufactured: (1) Projectors, (2) Screens, (3) Radio and/or television receivers, (4) Amplifiers, microphones and other sound equipment, (5) School sound systems.)

Company	Products
Admiral Corporation 3800 Cortland Street Chicago 47, Illinois	3, 4, 5
Altec Lansing Corporation 9356 Santa Monica Boulevard Beverly Hills, California	4
American Optical Company Instrument Division Buffalo 15, New York	1
Ampro Corporation 2835 North Western Avenue Chicago 18, Illinois	1
Atlas Sound Corporation 1451 Thirty-ninth Street Brooklyn, New York	4, 5
Automatic Projection Corporation 19 West Forty-fourth Street New York 18, New York	1
Avco Manufacturing Corporation Crosley Division 1329 Arlington Street Cincinnati 25, Ohio	3
Bausch and Lomb Optical Company 635 St. Paul Street Rochester, New York	1
Bell and Howell Company 7100 McCormick Road Chicago 45, Illinois	1
Bell Sound Systems, Inc. 555 Marion Road Columbus 7, Ohio	4, 5
Bendix Radio Radio and Television Division East Joppa Road Baltimore 4, Maryland	3
Charles Beseler Company 60 Badger Avenue Newark 8, New Jersey	1

David Bogen Company, Inc. 4, 5
29 Ninth Avenue
New York 14, New York

R.T. Bozak Company 4
90 Montrose Avenue
Buffalo, New York

Capehart-Farnsworth Corporation 3, 4
3700 East Pontiac Street
Fort Wayne 1, Indiana

Da-Lite Screen Company, Inc. 2
2711 North Pulaski Road
Chicago 39, Illinois

DeVry Corporation 1
1111 Armitage Avenue
Chicago, Illinois

DuKane Corporation 4, 5
St. Charles, Illinois

Allen B. DuMont Laboratories, Inc. 3
TV Receiver Sales Division
35 Market Street
East Paterson, New Jersey

Eastman Kodak Company 1
Rochester 4, New York

Electro-Voice, Inc. 4
Carroll and Cecil Streets
Buchanan, Michigan

Emerson Radio & Phonograph Corporation 3
111 Eighth Avenue
New York 11, New York

Freed Radio Corporation 3, 4
Educational Products Division
200 Hudson Street
New York 13, New York

General Electric Company 3, 4
Receiver Department
Electronics Division
Electronics Park
Syracuse 1, New York

GoldE Manufacturing Company 1
1214 – 22nd West Madison Street
Chicago 7, Illinois

Jensen Manufacturing Company 4
6601 South Laramie Avenue
Chicago 38, Illinois

Keystone Manufacturing Company 151 Hallett Street Boston 24, Massachusetts	1
LaBelle Industries, Inc. Oconomowoc, Wisconsin	1
James B. Lansing Sound, Inc. 2439 Fletcher Drive Los Angeles 39, California	4
The Magnavox Company 2131 Bueter Road Fort Wayne 4, Indiana	3, 5
Mark Simpson Manufacturing Company 32-28-49 Street Long Island City, New York	4, 5
Muntz TV, Inc. 1735 West Belmont Avenue Chicago 13, Illinois	3
Operadio Manufacturing Company St. Charles, Illinois	1, 3
Permoflux Corporation 4900 West Grand Avenue Chicago 39, Illinois	4
Philco Corporation Tioga and C Streets Philadelphia 34, Pennsylvania	3
Radiant Manufacturing Company 1201 South Talman Avenue Chicago 8, Illinois	2
Radio Corporation of America RCA Victor Division Front and Cooper Streets Camden, New Jersey	1, 3, 4, 5
The Rauland Corporation 4245 North Knox Avenue Chicago 41, Illinois	4, 5
Raven Screens Company Inc. 124 East 124th Street New York City	2
Reeves Soundcraft Corporation 10 East Fifty-second Street New York City	4
Shure Brothers, Inc. 225 West Huron Street Chicago 10, Illinois	4

Stromberg-Carlson Company 100 Carlson Road Rochester 3, New York	3, 4, 5
Sylvania Electric Products Inc. Radio & Television Division 254 Rano Street Buffalo 7, New York	3
Three Dimension Company 4555 West Addison Street Chicago 41, Illinois	1
The Turner Company 909 Seventeenth Street, Northwest Cedar Rapids, Iowa	4
University Loudspeakers Inc. 80 South Kensico Avenue White Plains, New York	4, 5
Utah Radio Products Company Inc. 1123 East Franklin Street Huntington, Indiana	4
Victor Animatograph Corporation Davenport, Iowa	1
Viewlex, Inc. Queens Boulevard Long Island City 1, New York	1
Vita-Lite Screen Company 239 A Street San Diego 1, California	
Webster-Chicago Corporation 5619 West Bloomingdale Chicago 39, Illinois	4
Webster Electric Company 1900 Clark Street Racine, Wisconsin	4, 5
Westinghouse Electric Corporation Television-Radio Division 1354 Susquehanna Avenue Sunbury, Pennsylvania	3
Zenith Radio Corporation 6001 Dickens Avenue Chicago 39, Illinois	3

For additional information consult:

"Annual Buyers' Guide Issue." *Electronics* Vol. 25, no. 6a, June 1952. McGraw-Hill Book Co., Inc., 330 West 42nd Street, New York 18, New York.

Audio-Visual Equipment Directory. National Audio-Visual Association, Inc., 845 Chicago Avenue, Evanston, Illinois.

"1953 Hemisphere and Station Studio Equipment Directory." *Tele-Tech* 11 (no. 11): 113-207; October 1952. Caldwell-Clements, Inc., 480 Lexington Avenue, New York 17, New York.

Membership List Trade Directory. Radio-Television Manufacturers Association, 777 Fourteenth Street, N.W., Washington 5, D.C.

Planning Schools For Use of Audio-Visual Materials -- No. 1 Classrooms. Department of Audio-Visual Instruction, National Education Association, 1201 16th Street, N.W., Washington, D.C. (Appendix contains a list of companies producing and/or distributing light control materials and equipment.)

Radio's Master. United Catalog Publishers, Inc., 106-110 Lafayette Street, New York 3, New York.

"Trade Directory Issue" (annual). *Radio and Television Retailing.* Caldwell-Clements, Inc., 480 Lexington Avenue, New York 17, New York.

PRICE LIST

Single copy..........................	$1.00
2 to 9 copies..........................	10% discount
10 to 99 copies......................	25% discount
100 and over..........................	33 1/3% discount

DEPARTMENT OF AUDIO-VISUAL INSTRUCTION

OFFICERS

President
JAMES W. BROWN
Supervisor, Instructional Materials Center, University of Washington

First Vice-President
PAUL W. F. WITT
Associate Professor of Education, Teachers College, Columbia University

Second Vice-President
HERBERT R. JENSEN
Director, Instructional Materials Center, Colorado State College of Education

Executive Secretary
J. J. McPHERSON
Director, Division of Audio-Visual Instructional Service, National Education Association

DELEGATES AT LARGE

LEE W. COCHRAN
Executive Assistant, Extension Division, State University of Iowa

A. J. FOY CROSS
Director, Center for Field Services, New York University

AMO DE BERNARDIS
Director, Instructional Materials Portland Public Schools, Oregon

CARLTON W. H. ERICKSON
Director, Audio-Visual Aids Center, University of Connecticut

LESLIE E. FRYE
Director, Divsioni of Visual Education, Cleveland Public Schools, Ohio

JOSEPH T. NERDEN
Consultant, Audio-Visual Education, Connecticut State Department of Education

FRANCIS W. NOEL
Chief, Bureau of Audio-Visual Education, California State Department of Education

CHARLES F. SCHULLER
Assistant Director, Bureau of Visual Instruction, University of Wisconsin

LELIA TROLINGER
Director, Bureau of Audio-Visual Instruction, University of Colorado

www.ingramcontent.com/pod-product-compliance
Lightning Source LLC
LaVergne TN
LVHW010549100826
845148LV00013B/2663

* 9 7 8 1 6 8 1 2 3 9 6 6 8 *